MARK MY WORDS

MARK MAZEIKA

Published 2024

Printed in the United States of America

First Edition

ISBN (softcover): 978-1-963380-43-9
ISBN (e-book): 978-1-963380-44-6

For information, address:

Holzer Books LLC
8 The Green, Ste. A
Dover, Delaware 19901 USA

For information about special discounts available for bulk purchases, sales promotions, and educational needs, contact:

info@holzerbooksllc.com
+1 (888) 901-7776

holzerbooksLLC©

CONTENTS

Spoken Words

Is my recollection of the events leading up to a poem true?

Probably not, what I know as truth, would not be the same as you.

My poetry is inspired by memories time has reimagined in my head,

They're meant to be spoken, and hopefully, they're captivating when read.

These poems are not vague, leaving little room for interpretation.

I want to remind others that we are all connected by similar situations.

I create poetry to make something tolerable out of situations that went another way.

Replacing ugliness with thoughts I can live with, but did not always convey.

I believe poetry should be inspired with a certain lyrical musicality;

I prefer it to rhyme, flow, and have a creative wit.

What I write, I usually refer to as "my words."

But if I have done my job, I've created poems, meant to be spoken and therefore heard.

My words may be sung like a ballad or read like a letter,

And if one day they became lyrics to a song, that's all the better.

The basis of these poems is usually a lost love, who harbors a different account of the tales I tell.

I have taken creative liberties because their renderings didn't end as well.

There are two sides to every story, but lucky for me you will only hear mine.

The narratives I create allow me to proceed forward, and not wallow behind.

Some of my poems are true, and others were sarcastically created.

I would not be forthcoming as to which category one falls if I were debated.

One thing we learn when dealing with affairs of the heart is never to kiss and tell,

I have chosen to record liaisons through poetry that ran parallel.

My words encapsulate circumstances that happened to me, once upon my time.

I have removed the names, and in doing so, I'm pretty sure I have removed the crime.

Mark my words, it is going to get dark in here, but do not be alarmed.

Only my feelings and nothing else was ever truly harmed.

As you read my words, you'll notice my flair for the dramatic has been initiated.

But you may also notice violence suggested in jest, and never tolerated.

Looking back, the occasional obscurity was responding to love with immaturity.

I am not usually inspired to write from a lighthearted frame of mind.

However, in my darkness, a life lesson and a poem may align.

So, change your recollection of any memory you can no longer bear.

Make something beautiful out of the ugliness that happened to you there.

Tweak your history to something that helps you get on with your life instead.

Let go of the stories trapped inside your head.

The same picture painted by one loving couple would never look the same.

But once the love is gone, what remains forever, depends on how it's framed.

Just like our lives, poetry can go askew;

but how you write the beginning, middle, and end is up to you.

I embellish the light, yet out of darkness I write, which has made me seem profound.

So read on, look at the pieces of my broken heart that I was able to scrape off the ground.

But that's how it goes, right? When we play with others' emotions, hearts are going to be broken.

And contained here are the only reflections that will ever be spoken.

Unforgiven
A Letter to Love

My clumsy emotions tripped at your feet, scattered and reckless, I knew I'd been beat.

You busted my ribs to uncage my heart, now leaving me for dead to find a new start.

I am unforgiven, from your point of view; I am no longer fit for living, at least not with you.

Where does one start, when they do not understand their part?

Where does one begin, when they feel they're at their end?

I haven't the face to stand before yours and say all of the hurt I am hurting today.

I cannot believe you would not bend to my persistence.

I haven't the strength to equal your resistance, and I cower to the whore I've become, expressing my thoughts, which now seem so dumb.

I realize you have made up your mind, to leave both me and our life behind.

Where does one begin, when they feel they're at their end?

Where does one save me, when I have become a wreck emotionally?

And where does one find me, when I have been scarred romantically?

And finally,

Upon reading this, if you should ever change your mind,

Remember, I was hiding in places only you were able to find.

So if you have a change of heart...I guess I'll be waiting at the start.

LIARS

We are liars and we probably deserve each other; that's just our fate.

But I do not want you any more than you want me, so let us take a moment to deliberate.

There is so much more that we could say, but neither of us wants to talk.

You had me feeling something, so I didn't want to walk.

I could have told you where this was going, but at the time I wanted to go.

I cannot listen to you anymore; here is what I think, therefore, this is what I know.

We are liars and we lie to each other, that's just what we do.

We don't recognize each other, and soon we'll ask, "Who the hell are you?"

Neither of us could care less, so we might as well go.

If this was ever bearable, well that was long ago.

After what I have seen, you're lucky I did not already flee.

For I have seen things, a man was never meant to see.

I will take the lead and take all my things.

I'll leave you untied and without any strings.

I'd like to say that I wish you the best and I hope that your life ends up great,

but you'll wonder if that's the truth or another hidden message for you to translate.

I Am the Fly

I am the fly who has eaten enough of your shit;

I know you better than you'd like to admit.

Hanging around on the walls, I've heard things I shouldn't.

Now you worry I'll repeat secrets I wouldn't.

I'll buzz around, unaware I am annoying you.

Your paranoia will dictate what you will do.

I know how this goes: you'll sneak up from behind,

and you will kill me, for your own peace of mind.

LEFT FOR UNDEAD

My heart was severed like a weed from the lawn.

You were unaware of the roots you had tugged upon.

What you unearthed was the lifeline connecting you to me.

I succumbed to a rush of blood brought on by love's brutality.

When I came to, the soothing sound of unseen insects replaced my missing heartbeat.

I knew my world was different because I no longer felt complete.

None of this was how I envisioned my last day.

I anticipated being surrounded by loved ones as I peacefully slipped away.

But earlier you arrived, armed with ammunition in the form of bullet points to say.

You were my life; you told me we're done...I died that day.

People come and go and they take a piece of us with them when they leave.

My body was dismembered; leaving only my shadow to grieve.

Perhaps it was the finality of what was said.

Your intent was not to kill me, just that my heart be misled.

I once lived in the light of your love; now banished to the dark orbit of your sun.

It may have been more humane had your bullet points been fired from a gun.

Dreams once spoken, festered into a nightmare as I awoken to find I'd been left undead.

I live amongst the lonely, yet the people we once were, refuse to evacuate my head.

I resurrected in a familiar park; dispelling all belief my eternity would be somewhere much

higher.

I am now laying down roots on the side of a road, where traffic lights still hang from a wire.

My life expectancy expects me to live on, but I can barely walk as I'm looked upon with dread,

I'm thought to be spiteful because I can't move on; believing no better love is up the road ahead.

That which didn't kill me has done so partially.

Now I wander around, with the wonder of when I'll be put in the ground.

I've become heartless, with a need to do unto others. For without love, who cares about lovers?

This was an apparent wound to the heart, but in reality, my heart is gone.

A doctor would tell me, "You can live without it, you'll be fine, get dressed, and carry on."

Though not a rare condition and it has been seen before.

It is only fatal if you ignored the early warning signs; that you fell in love with a whore.

Hiding in the shadows of love, my questions continue to compound.

How did I awaken that evening and why am I still above ground?

The secrets we bury eventually grow, but I cannot bloom until I'm six feet below.

I disagree with the results of their findings that dreadful night.

Something about their forensics didn't seem quite right.

They were unwilling to pronounce me dead, but I sure can.

Nobody is questioning the "how," but I'm disputing the "when."

That was the day my life ended. Eight o'clock was the time of death.

Though it is believed to be inconclusive until I draw my final breath.

I put my heart out there, so I have no one but myself to blame.

I can no longer say, "I know in my heart," but if I could, I'd proclaim...

"I died at age thirty"...just not quite enough for me to get dirty.

THE AFTER TASTE

Once upon a time, but the second time was twice as bad.

The third time was not a charm; we just drove each other mad.

I guess there could be such a thing as love at first sight,

but we were cursed with less love with each passing night.

If dreams really do come true, so does the nightmare of waking up next to you.

Our lesson was learned; the flame blew out, but it was fun while it burned.

Let's wrap up this happily ever after, because "happily" doesn't describe what existed.

We'll leave knowing one day we will feel less bitter, less twisted.

They say there are books that state fairy tales really can come true.

I can honestly say I didn't bother to read them, and neither did you.

When we are not with each other, we are much more upstanding people.

Then we get back together and, well, you know what they say about the sequel.

For a long, long time, we fight and disagree more than we cherish and love, love.

But what went wrong? Select the option "All of the Above."

So, to you, I say, "happily ever after, and all its aftertaste."

We've come to find our time together was merely just a waste.

A Tale in Two Poems

Oblivion, U.S.

The bomb at the bank.

The fireworks over the pavilion.

Welcome to Oblivion!

Current Events Claudia crawls through town.

She won't stand for that which she cannot sit through.

But she'll get around and speak up for the ADA.

And she'll stop at the Chinese restaurant.

Talk is cheap, hearing it's cheaper;

seeing is believing...the fortune cookies will guide the way.

Deadeye Darren drove by too.

He doesn't see how people can be so blind.

But bring your gun if you're coming for his he will remind.

And he'll stop by the gypsy fortune teller.

Talk is cheap, hearing it's cheaper;

seeing is believing...the crystal ball will guide the way.

Holy Holly fell to her knees.

She'll pray for those who don't share her beliefs.

She's seen the light and now believes in every individuals' religious rights.

And sometime today she'll go to mass at the chapel.

Talk is cheap, hearing it's cheaper;

seeing is believing...the word of God will guide the way.

Dopey David's keeping it sober.

He no longer performs his magic tricks.

He won't shoot up or score for kicks.

There's nothing up his sleeve, so if he stops at the drugstore, it won't be to get high.

Talk is cheap, hearing it's cheaper,

seeing is believing...the magic eight ball will guide the way.

Jester Justin rode in on a float.

He doesn't understand why everyone can't be proud, he'll quote.

But he'll stop at the parade and spill some tea.

Talk is cheap, hearing it's cheaper;

seeing is believing...the tea leaves will guide the way.

BLM were also there to remind everyone their lives matter too.

In the first place, they will no longer be made to feel they are second place.

All they ask is to be treated equally in the eyes of all, including the law.

Talk is cheap, hearing it's cheaper;

seeing is believing...nobody should be above or below the law.

And that will govern and guide the way.

Look beyond what people tell you is true, and listen to how they feel.

Palm the pavement with your ear to the ground.

There's plenty of speech but nobody hears the sound.

With all the hustle and bustle of these New York streets,

There, standing in the harbor, Lady Liberty weeps.

She knows the talk is cheap and the actions may be more difficult.

But Liberty will guide our way, as she is very wise.

For she knows when people come together, a United States will be the prize.

Put down the put-downs meant towards others.

Every citizen should be respected, they are our brothers.

We can learn from the diverse representation of our military corps;

they stand as one to confront our enemies abroad and win wars.

The vets counted on each other to go into battle and get the job done.

If we don't adopt their mentality here, nothing will be won.

We each get one go-around to make our life the best.

Some believe God placed us here as part of his test.

Remember, it is not our place to pass judgment on the rest.

God created all, therefore all are blessed.

So show some compassion toward those trying to write a better memoir.

And let's be reminded our flag did not begin with 50 stars.

Until we are united there will be protests in the street...

Where these groups hope everyone will come to meet...

To hear about and support their cause...

Join them, their desire for change deserves our applause.

So, goodbye to Oblivion!

We need to rethink everything we've been taught that led to hatred.

As citizens of the United States, we should feel obligated.

Unite, not fight, and let's try to understand each other's plight.

And we should be happy to oblige.

READY AND WAITING

Ready to go, waiting patiently to leave.

I was out too late, waiting on something to believe.

Ready for bed but waiting for you to arrive.

One drink after another, I thought we would never leave that dive.

We weren't ready to pass in the night but should have waited to set sail.

These two ships should have up and left after one cocktail.

Instead, we decided, "Let's knock a few more back."

Ready to indulge, waiting to add liquor instead of subtract.

Ready to move on but waiting to kiss.

We figured we'd have a toast and see what could become of this.

Wait, we're probably going down the wrong path.

We know this won't work, just not ready to do the math.

Regardless, we were ready to try and we were waiting to hear the band.

We were both being stupid and we had no reservations beforehand.

Ready for whatever, waiting to get busy.

Wait, hold up, I am drunk, and you are getting a little frisky.

You were like, "Come here, take a swig, this is really lousy."

Waiting to go, ready for bed, now I am starting to get drowsy.

I don't do shots, but I took a bullet for the team.

Ready to take off, but waiting for the liquor to pass through our bloodstream.

Being responsible, you said you'd call and get us each separate rides.

Ready to call it a night, but we left together. Were you surprised?

Waiting to face the facts, not ready to admit this was a mistake until later today.

But I'm already planning my escape, wait 'til you're asleep, then make my shameful getaway.

It's Complicated

I woke up today in last night's clothes, thinking I was late for tomorrow's plans.

I don't remember what went on last night, but at least today I remember it's not yet tomorrow.

It's very likely that tomorrow I'll wake up in today's clothes and think it's last night again.

Because I'll probably be wearing the clothes I had on last night again tomorrow, unless I can do the wash today.

Don't worry, sometime today I'll remember what I did last night, and I can fill you in tomorrow.

But tomorrow, don't ask me what I did last night (meaning today), because, well...

It's complicated.

Last night I dreamt that tomorrow was great, but if that's true, I wouldn't know that today.

I think I told you last night that sometime today we would make plans for tomorrow.

But before you woke up today, it dawned on me that I have plans for tomorrow with someone else I met last night.

Don't get me wrong, last night was fun, but tomorrow is out of the question, and today...I believe you think I was a mistake.

By the way, you told me your name last night, and I said I won't remember it tomorrow.

Well, here we are today.

UNEASY

Our hearts beat faster in time with our eyes.

Our stomachs flutter with the same butterflies.

This could be the beginning, where everything is new.

I would like to take the time to get to know you.

Sure, I am nervous, and it would be easier to leave.

We could both go home, but what would that achieve?

We would continue to be alone and never know the unknown.

We should give this a try and become at ease with the uneasy.

Even if our butterflies are starting to make us feel queasy.

What do you think? I'm going to need you to formulate the words.

Because up until now, what you are thinking has been unheard.

Do you want me to go, or do you want me to stay?

Okay, if you're sure that is what you want, I will not delay.

ALWAYS WATCHING

I know when you are near; of that, I am always aware.

My hope is you do not feel the pressure of my stare.

And if you'd give me some time out of your day,

I could approach without fear of being turned away.

In contrast to you, I feel unclean; I don't mean dirty-minded.

I cannot realize any of your flaws; I guess I've been blinded.

I am watching you, and I like when we start talking.

My hope is you do not perceive it as stalking.

You can brighten my day with anything you have to say;

Then my day will darken when my thoughts get deep and go astray.

I will analyze everything I did or didn't say once the conversation stops and we go on our way.

Every word you said, will linger in my head.

In my mind, I will replay and wonder: did I choke or did I blunder?

There may be a next time when I can get the words out,

that will let you know what I've been feeling throughout.

I need a little more confidence to match who I think you are.

I don't want you to look at me and think I'm bizarre.

Who am I kidding and what does it matter?

I will take whatever time you can spare and listen to your chatter.

I will listen to you as you continue talking, then I will scamper away and continue my stalking.

EYE WITNESS

I do not hold you in contempt, in the courtroom of my stare.

You will not find judgement from me there.

For these are my eyes, and if they turn from you, it's meaningless.

They are not my emotions you are witnessing.

You would have to look elsewhere to see their evidence.

I hold them in my heart, close to me: Exhibit "A."

If they were to be released from their chamber—

it would be apparent, for they would expose me—all of me—and consume you.

So, do not look for me behind my lashes.

It will not be my eyes that drop the gavel here today.

It will not be "a look" that prosecutes you in these hearings.

My gaze will not pass judgment.

But it is my heart, which you cannot see;

and my heart is the only eyewitness to your crime.

And it is my heart that will render its verdict on you today.

You have been sentenced to a life without me, for my lesson was learned.

This court can now be adjourned.

UNTIL DEATH

I had the paperwork drawn up, before a new love came.

I knew you would feel, I thought you were to blame.

I didn't, but suddenly I didn't hate you enough.

I decided to leave when things got too rough.

Everyone eventually gets married, but half experience the pain of divorce,

where they will be financially ruined and have their lives go off course.

Your feelings and my feelings were never the same.

Our love was vulnerable and, unexpectedly, a new love came.

Hatred was festering as we pulled out our knives.

One of us needed to get out, to save both of our lives.

Since the commitments we made on our wedding day laid out a timeframe,

something was destined to get deadly before that time came.

So I am not the hero, seeking his moment of glory.

But our tale could have concluded with a murder mystery story.

Neither version of our story will be any good.

Looking back, I think we would have done things differently if we could.

But with no sickness or health issues in sight, leaving was the better solution for sure.

Because when we said, "Until death, do us part," well that may have been a bit premature.

COME UPSTAIRS

I don't need a nap.

I want a nightcap; you're my sweet Lullaby.

Just a long night of sleep, one that makes me count sheep.

Tonight you need to know me, you need to know my cares.

Tonight you need to know me, come upstairs.

Tonight you need to feel me, you have known a boyish bore.

Tonight you need to feel me, come up and close the door.

Tonight you'll need to bathe me, you'll need to wash my hair.

Tonight you need to hold me, and prove to me you care.

Come upstairs, sweet Lullaby, and please don't try to flee.

It's late and time to solidify just what you mean to me.

Come upstairs, we are both alone,

And if you agree, we may be able to see our way out of the friend's zone.

On Second Thought...

Given the chance to do it all over, would I know what to do?

"Had I only known" I ponder, as I think this through.

Would I be ready to do it all over again?

But what do I know now that I didn't know then?

I can see the path right in front of me.

Yet, I still don't know what to do with this opportunity.

I may have missed making that one simple change;

therefore, a redo would not rearrange.

And is there any guarantee I'd be better for it?

Life turned out good and I am one of the fortunate.

There's something to be said as second chances are sought;

count your blessings and the good fortune you've been brought.

The good in my life has outweighed the bad.

The anger within doesn't make me that mad.

I may have stumbled along the way but in the end, I made out fine.

I gave back the negativity, I didn't want it, it wasn't mine.

Dreaming of what "could have been" is just a distraction.

If offered a second chance, I'd follow the same course of action.

Go Easy on Me

Go easy on me when you go.

Try not to let your misplaced love for me show.

Don't tell me you love me because we both know you don't.

But don't ask me to stop loving you, because we both know I won't.

The clock has run out, and you've decided we're done.

You have realized, for you, I was not the right one.

You've abandoned this relationship and can no longer commit.

I know what is about to happen, so go on, don't prolong it.

I don't have the strength for what you're about to say, so be kind.

Take my heart into consideration and keep my love in mind.

If we never speak again, leave with something nice to say;

smile, be sweet, then go on your way.

Nothing else matters to me except everything you think of me.

So choose the right words and we can end this amicably.

This will be more difficult for me, I can tell.

You will be able to move on and I won't handle it well.

My heart is breaking, but that is no reason for you to stay.

My coping mechanisms will have me believe that you will return one day.

But for now, it is going to be the death of me to watch as you go.

I would never let you see it and I forbid to let it show.

But, I don't see how I'll get through this nor handle the sorrow.

Because speaking for me, without you, there can be no tomorrow.

THE RODENT IN ME

Drink from me and my vine of life.

Handle me in ways that promise me I have risen above the others,

and I am blessed amongst men.

If I have the power to offer you a new life and all of eternity:

shouldn't I be able to stand before you and say, "I am powerless without you"?

You will breathe through my lungs from this night forward.

Be gentle with me and the flow of my heart; it has been shut in for centuries.

Never wandering out into the sun-drenched sky.

Destined to bleed for eternity in the black of nowhere.

For I have been living off the blood of another for many a night,

and my hands have been soiled, my lips have been stained

and I fear my heart is pumping too hard to ever restart.

I have been damned to feed from the jugulars of others.

Which makes me vulnerable in ways I am not accustomed to.

And you, and I, have been using our minds to cut each other's throats.

Carefully playing with tactics, until we found the one which hurts.

And I have been skillfully manipulating you, and you have witnessed, I am my heart;

sickened and vulnerable since I made you a part of this.

I, the passionate prince, will bend over the sleeping wreckage I have made of your body.

I will love you tonight, but only tonight.

Then I will flutter away before sunrise.

Like the rodent I am, and the one you will become, by the time I finish with you.

CHECKMATE

Checkmate, your move; as for your gameplay, I approve.

But it wasn't checkers we came here to play.

And I removed the pieces standing in my way.

In case you weren't aware, we came to play chess.

I'm going to take out your king and clean up your mess.

Checkers is for children; this game requires skill.

I removed your protection and placed you at a standstill.

I went to combat with each of your pawns and took out the whole battalion.

During that skirmish, we also saw the demise of one of your stallions.

Regarding your bishops, now they took a little more fight,

moving diagonally across the battlefield, trying to escape their plight.

There has been plenty of property damage to both of your castles.

That was pretty straightforward and not much of a hassle.

Lastly, I jumped in the saddle to joust with your final knight.

God rest his soul, he will be needing the bishop's prayers tonight.

We're almost alone, it's your move, and I can wait all day.

You don't want to quit now, after all, you came to play.

Checkmate, concentrate; make your move if you got one left in you.

Your King is the last piece in our way, shall we bid him adieu?

DETHRONED

Hear ye, Hear ye,

The king would like to be alone.

Hear ye, Hear ye,

The queen must now leave the throne.

Once upon a time, but now is the time to leave.

The queen is thought to have practiced sorcery to deceive.

Whilst you cross the moat, milady,

watch the alligators shan't bite your ass.

I will not come on horseback with a slipper made of glass.

Head straight through the forest and watch out for those sheep.

They are often just wolves looking for fair maidens to reap.

Though you once were a fair maiden and then a beloved queen,

one would not describe you as fair, had they known what the king had seen.

On second thought, may you stay for a fortnight?

I shan't rely on gators and wolves, to do what I feel is just and right.

I will deal with this the best way I know how.

No trial would be fair for a maiden whose not,

no head would be needed, for a queen, whose vows she has forgot.

THE LIFE OF MY
BATTERY

I think I forgot to allow my brain to charge last night.

I'm awake, but nothing about me feels quite right.

My full potential will not be realized as my hands, tongue, and brain all seem enlarged.

What good am I going to be if I'm not fully charged?

It's not like me to forget such things.

I hope I get through the day; but let's see what it brings.

When my battery's life has come to its end,

I no longer get reception, and I can't comprehend.

Tonight, I will get charged up and get plenty of rest.

Maybe tomorrow, I will be able to accept a simple friend request.

FROM HEREAFTER

Wake up today, child, though the moon is still here.

Something's gone wrong, and the sun won't appear.

You say you've seen God and all that He's done,

He can fish with no rod and make loaves out of one.

In a time, in the worlds, from Eden to here,

Relinquished of questions that now seem so clear.

Wake up today, child, and be on your best,

For God has granted you eternal rest.

SOMETIME BETWEEN DUSK AND DAWN

The television burned out like a candle as my spirit fell asleep.

My daily work and commitments were done, and suddenly I cried.

Sunrise will start the repetition, though it will seem less fun.

The cry is still there, thirty years later, alone again.

My work must continue; the motivation is money.

Sunrise starts it, sunset ends it, and some rest will help this evening.

I won't worry about a thing, for I'll have dreams of you.

I don't remember the dream actually ending...

But sometime between dusk and dawn, I was thrown into today's reality.

The nightmare starts it, because you ended it.

Clawing frantically at the satin edge of a blanket strangling my body.

Sweating feverishly as I slid atop the bed; trying to muster the strength to remove you

from my head. I was unsuccessful.

Choking on words I never said, looking for light the darkness could not shed.

Scrambling for a love, which has obviously fled.

Cutting my eyes just so they'd open; breaking my heart, because it still hoping,

that you didn't really leave me today, and I didn't stand there with nothing to say.

If I could sleep through the night little people, it will all be better in the new light of day.

Oh, how powerful the night, when I am left alone to analyze my fright.

THE ONE THAT GOT TO STAY

It turns out all the ones that got away are now sorely missed.

Yet you, the one that got to stay, have me aggravated and pissed.

With you it's one thing after another: cry, complain, and nag.

I know the person you could be and chose to ignore the red flags.

You hear the things I say, but not the way they were intended.

I get so twisted and confused and wonder why you're so offended.

I never said I wouldn't miss you... All I said is, I didn't want to kiss you.

And I never said I didn't think you were pretty... All I said is I feel shitty...

When I'm with you, I never know what to do.

I guess I should ask myself "did I do something wrong?"

No, fuck that, it's your game, but I'll come along.

You constantly stand around and criticize... If you were wise...

You would take my advice, and every now and then...say something nice.

If that is how it has to be for me to stay committed to you;

I will spend my lifetime trying to see things from your point of view.

So I guess I will join you in these vicious games we'll play.

Who knows, maybe I will start becoming agreeable and not disobey.

I've come to realize we both love the fight; maybe it is what keeps us together despite...

The fact that most of the time, you get on my nerves,

Maybe this is all the two of us deserve.

We are destined to continue arguing, it is just in our genes.

Oh, Christ, I think I know what this means?

We will be yelling, screaming, and complaining for the rest of our lifetime.

I think this means we are going to love each other, now and for the rest of time.

WICKED

You are even more wicked than the rest.

The covens have spoken in all directions: you're the best.

Grab your broomstick and head toward the south.

I cannot stand the immoral things that come out of your mouth.

I cannot believe so I am willing to guess,

You will be banished in the south, so from there continue your journey west.

There has been too much sorcery that I just didn't see.

All your hocus-pocus and you don't feel the least bit guilty.

I have no more time for what has come to be,

you have cast too many spells of which we will never agree.

Instead of all of this black magic and the vicious back and forth,

when you finish poisoning the west coast, head up north

I wondered how you came to be this deceiving and mean.

One day you will be celebrated and hailed as the Wicked Queen.

Your ugly warts have exposed how evil you are, to say the least.

When you leave the north it's a quick trip, but be sure to fly east.

So get going, be gone... fly, up, up, and away!

Be sure to visit Salem, where the fires of Hell await your decay.

COME WHAT MAY

Today is another warm *August* day in *November*.

It's difficult to predict the forecast as we *March* into *December*.

Come to think, *July* was a bit cooler this year, and *October* was warmer than usual.

And still, they claim the changing weather patterns aren't provable.

In all likelihood, *January* will feel much like *September*.

And *February* will never be as cold as I remember.

The extreme weather is becoming more threatening, not so much here in the East.

In comparison to the South and out West, our frequency is least.

Will springtime temperatures still begin in *April* and end in *June*?

Probably not, if we don't start controlling the climate soon!

We all need to do our part, and not continue taking it day by day.

Our planet deserves a better solution than, "it is what it is" or ... "come what *May.*"

My Excuse for My Self-Abuse

Fetch me a shot of your finest poison, then roll the barrel over my head.

I thought I could bury my feelings and take them with me when I'm dead.

Get the car and finish the job; that's where I've been driven.

If this is going to kill me, for this I'd be forgiven.

My penchant for inflicting pain on myself is getting way too rough;

it has proven unsuccessful; perhaps I haven't done enough.

I ran with scissors and cut my nose off to spite my face.

I saw things much clearer, once I sprayed my eyes with mace.

Now I'll never have to look at you, ever again.

I've tried to walk away, but chose to hurt myself instead.

I've cut off my arms, so I'd never again desire to hold you.

My self-harm has no limits, and there is so much more I can do.

This is going to end badly, and that is coming from someone who is not the brightest fella.

Hand me that rope, I want to try something, I'll be in the cellar.

I can't tell you how many times I had to bite my tongue, just to give you a kiss.

Well actually I could, I kept count right here on my wrists.

Don't get me wrong, I don't blame you for my self-abuse.

But get the bolt cutters from the shed and cut me loose

What was I thinking, the basement ceiling isn't as tall as that tree.

Even my suffering has had it with me, getting the best of me.

I don't want to permanently cripple myself, with my constant abuse.

So it may be best that I walk away and we call it a truce.

One stone can kill two birds, and spare the death of me.

I have to convince myself that I actually want to be set free.

I can give it a try, I can walk away, and hope that this is finally the end.

I've looked at our world through rose-colored glasses for as long as I can.

But regardless of how I was looking at it, I was still seeing red.

I'm out of here. One day this may all seem okay.

Can you put the chainsaw back in the shed?

The Question

One question will show you just how much I care.

I am committed to proving to you that I will always be there.

Held in your heart where I hope to stay, a little nervous with something to say.

Respectfully down on my knee asking for your hand in marriage: will you marry me?

Let's start our forever, beginning here today.

You had my heart; now take my hand and become my fiancée.

Standing here in a tux, with nothing up my sleeve, I hope you understand...

That with this ring I promise we will have everything we've planned.

And if you will have and hold me, forever as we will have agreed.

We shall be newlyweds and our souls will proceed.

Our love will let nothing get in our way.

Now that you've said yes, "I Do" was the only thing left to say.

So let's start our forever, on this our wedding day.

THE GHOST IN ME

Ordinarily, I do not believe in ghosts, but happily, our souls did meet.

You appeared before me that day when destiny introduced us on the street.

The ghost in you flew through the spirit in me and promised me you'd stay.

I brought you into my house, and it became less haunted that day.

It was both spooky and eerie, but I knew we were meant to be together.

And it became my place to love and protect you forever.

It was inevitable that our spirits would come to haunt each other.

The ghost in you could not have summoned more love from another.

You allowed me to care for and look after you, the best I can.

We were two feral souls with the same needs, but that was then.

I was meant to be your guy and for me, you were the only one that would do.

Immediately we sensed it was a good fit and from that moment I knew...

That the ghost of you has become entangled in all the veins that make up my heart.

One day you will break it, but for now, it would be too delicate to separate or take apart.

Like a stray that evening I may have rescued you, but you were the one who saved me.

I am now possessed by the ghost in you, where you will beat in my heart for eternity.

SMOKED

Go! Butt believe this is more difficult for me than for you.

For fourteen years I've considered you my friend.

I am through with you now, so go!

Some said I was addicted to you.

And we both know that was true.

Butt I will no longer let you get the best of me...

And that is exactly what you will do.

Please support me in this and go!

You will not be easily replaced.

I will not forget how you were there when I needed you.

Butt I am taking back control of my life.

Taking a deep breath for the first time in a long time.

Tossing out the ashes and remains of you, so go!

I'm starting a clean life with friends who will help me feel good about myself.

Those who will support me, as I need them.

This has been sincerely one-sided and has cost me so much.

Friends like you come and go and take a piece of you with them.

However, for the last time I have sucked the life from you, butt it was only my life.

And I no longer need you...so please go!

I Recognize

It takes all that I have to get out of bed.

I am not looking forward to what lies ahead.

I will make no one's day; nobody cares if they see me.

The only guarantee today is that no one will need me.

I have spent quite some time minding my business;

I have been counted out, which was not done on purpose.

I guess I've given the signals to leave me alone; no one will bother with me today,

And I fear my life has begun to go astray.

No party invitations or dinner reservations, questions, answers, or meaningful conversations.

An occasional "hello" or "how have you been" is all I may get, which by no means is a win.

My life is too short to be so content, to bore so much time which might well be spent.

Never expressing myself or the various sides of me, the caring person I know I could be.

The side which loves family and friends with a heart that awaits,

and not the person to which no one relates.

So please get to know me and give me a chance.

Please help fill my head and heart with romance.

Help me find friends who want me to be...a part of their lives they'd never set free.

Up until now, I fear that they see none of the traits I recognize in me.

Though I refuse to count myself out just yet, I will attempt to avoid any more regret.

And I hope that someone is up the road ahead that will give me the reason to get out of bed.

THE GUNSLINGER

I am the gunslinger, clenching a loaded revolver of dangerous emotions.

The safety is off, the chamber is full, and you are no longer protected by my devotion.

My thoughts, my words, and my reactions discharge like bullets,

Leaving shotgun shells all over for your forensics.

I am so far gone, ready to aim, shoot, and take you down.

I have you in my sights; you should probably run and take cover.

You are my target, but I don't care; I'll take out you or your new lover.

I am the gunslinger and you put me in a horrible position.

I am out of my mind with plenty of ammunition.

Tonight I am coming for you with resentment blazing.

Although I am barely holding it together, my mood is pretty amazing.

You brought stupidity to this gunfight, but I am down for the duel.

And since I am not in stable condition, let's assume I won't follow any rule.

I may come at you like a sniper, so you should hide or run far.

This may be a drive-by if I can borrow someone's car.

Nothing you say now can trigger my thoughts back into place.

I'm looking down the barrel and I only see your face.

You should have never gone and got inside my head.

It is full of evil intent, and someone could end up dead.

DARKCIDE

Thank you for giving me a moment of your time this evening; you may call me DarkCide.

I'd like to give you an update on what I have done up until now and what it is I have tried.

I have currently removed any happiness from your life to make you feel everything has been denied.

I have placed unbearable challenges in front of you, hoping I could help you decide.

Yet you do not appreciate my offer to come with me and leave all of this behind.

I have blocked out any sunlight and left only the darkness in your mind.

If you can find the strength you can actually escape me, the truth is I am you.

But I was hoping together we could come to an agreement to see this thing through.

Why have you not yet sold your soul to me?

I have invested the time and nothing in this world is free.

I am looking for my fee and I need you to pay and pay dearly.

I have placed obstacles in your path to help you find your way over to me.

And when you did not bend I enlisted my online minions as an added guarantee.

They aided me in manipulating every thought, emotion, and feeling you had.

Hoping the fruits of my labor would make you and your world feel really, really sad.

I put in the time and was determined to see you become tattered and torn.

I used all my power to see to it you were left crippled, weary, and worn.

Yet somehow you found the strength; leading you to believe you can get through all of this.

What gives you the right to change your mind? Follow as I reminisce....

You have come to the realization that these are temporary problems that you despise.

And you no longer hate the person in the mirror that you see with your own eyes.

If I still have not caused you to feel you are less than, well then I have failed.

You must continue our plan, you don't get to be the one who bailed.

It is getting late, and I'd like to leave knowing that your part of this endeavor has been completed.

We agreed it must be by your hands that one of us must come to an end or be defeated.

I came here to take you from this world regardless of family commitments and demands.

But this enlightenment you have had no longer responds to my commands.

For now, you have found your way out of this escape I have prepared for you.

I guess my time here is done, I tip my hat to the victor; you've truly had a breakthrough.

Your courage seems to have taken you off-page and helped you rewrite your story.

Continue your fight, keep me on my side, stay on yours, and walk away with this new-found glory.

OUR FAMILY TREE

As the uncertainty of the next week shades your face from the sun.

Leaving you feeling alone, under this tree, scared, and wanting to run.

Remember you are beginning this journey under our family tree.

Where you are safe and looked after by all, especially your husband and me.

Now go ahead and get going, all the while knowing...

That this is what is meant to be, for on the other side awaits your first baby.

It is true, this is all on you at this particular stage of the plan.

We are here to support you in spirit, the best that we can.

For you are about to bring another ornament to our tree.

So go on and get started; we are all excited, take your time, but hurry.

Remember that we are here for you, as you have been for us, or more personally, for me.

Time is wasting and this is the best part and it is going to be heavenly.

Start climbing, when you get to the part of the tree where the branches get thinner, sparse, and frail,

It won't be easy but remember that this end is the beginning of a new tale.

In the form of that someone you were looking for, and have now found.

With you and your husband, this child's life will be safe and sound.

This little someone that the sun just kissed; who in turn is now searching for you.

Crawling through the foliage, looking, screaming, and trying to get through.

And this time it is not us you will hear yelling sister, wife, daughter, or friend,

It will be someone from above yelling "mommy" for the first time until your lives end.

So go finish this phase of your journey and get to the top where the little branches start.

Bring down your first child for us to meet; you can carry her down in your heart.

Under her bark will be a great foundation; personality, wisdom, and character far beyond the rings on the base of our tree.

She will be loving when you teach her to love, and she can't help but be lovely.

She will be determined when you teach her, her drive and her purpose, and each day become more alive.She will be fearless when you teach her self-worth, and we will celebrate the day of her birth.

Moreover, she will grow tall from your example and the seeds you have planted.

Through all we will teach her, we can only hope that her life will be enchanted.

So go, begin your climb, the only direction I can give is you must go up and look toward the sun

or moon until you find the one that is destined to be yours, so keep an open mind.

Whether it is daybreak or nightfall is irrelevant, for that will be your sunlight or your moonlight,

that will shine in your heart forever, as you have in mine.

ALONE ON DATE NIGHT

We had plans to meet at my place hours ago.

After several attempts to contact you, you still didn't show.

Should I be concerned, or are you running late?

Is my schedule clear, or should I continue to wait?

I worried something might have happened to you.

I kept checking my phone, but no call came through.

If nothing's wrong, I've waited too long.

It's now after nine, and something tells me you're fine.

As the night passes by, so do the plans I had for us tonight.

Your actions will speak louder than an alibi that is airtight.

You said you wanted to come over, but it looks like you don't.

I'm not sure I want you to, in fact, I'm hoping you won't.

What was this all about? Why did you say you wanted to hang out?

Honestly, I stopped caring when you weren't here by ten.

Not sure how I'll react if I ever see you again.

I'm done waiting, it is now after eleven.

The face on that clock has berated me since seven.

I'd be crazy to think you were running late with not so much as a call.

But I could no longer listen to another tick of the clock on that wall.

The passing of time prohibits keeping any hope alive.

My self-esteem will not accept what you've contrived.

This side of you I did not see at the start.

You know nothing about me, so I won't take it to heart.

Being without a date-on-date night, allowed me the time to think about this logically.

But it is well past midnight and that is no longer resolved with an apology.

I'll leave a light on because I'm heading to bed.

I do hope you're okay, but this has really fucked with my head.

2:00 AM

Our standards fall with our pants to the floor as the lonely look to be alone no more.

Hoping to find what love looks for, yet making decisions based on physical allure.

We realize this once we arise: that as darkness fell, we fell for lies.

Decisions made at two in the morning should have come as our first warning.

But things are never quite as they seem, as morning breaks our self-esteem.

Reminding us that we should not delight in the fools we became under the cover of night.

Baggage Claim

I can be very demanding, which requires your accommodations to be more understanding.

I need someone who can clear the runway for an approaching fight.

Someone who will land the plane when there's turbulence on the flight.

You must go along with my itinerary, though it will probably be tough.

I've claimed all of my baggage, but I am dealing with some pretty old stuff.

I think the travel companion that could be the perfect fit,

is a concierge, who understands I am still dealing with some shit.

It isn't going to be a vacation if you stay here with me,

but everything is included, at no extra fee.

So, if this is the destination getaway you had in mind, and still want to give it a chance;

remember, I come with a lot of baggage, and it's likely I forgot to pack any romance.

I am Your
Reflection

Your existence is everywhere, yet they do not see you there.

Your story has been manipulated, agreed upon, and contemplated.

They look to me for proof that you're still here.

We must look inside ourselves, for that is where you appear.

Everything I am is because of you, yet I'd be nothing if your word is not true.

Sometimes the truth gets sugar-coated with glaze.

The shiny objects deceive us in unbecoming ways.

I seek your guidance in all I do, I pretend not to know, but I already knew.

Every time I hid, feeling lost or alone, you've led me to you, through the light you have shone.

When I lost my way or had any doubt, I counted on you and figured it out.

You have altered my journey to help me achieve the life I have refined.

I've become accustomed to your generosity and now feel less confined.

You have resuscitated my existence and that is where you end and I start.

Perhaps I have unblocked a vessel that has led me to a special place in your heart.

Every time I question if "ever-after" is the beginning of after or the ever of end;

I am reminded I've put my trust in you when I could not comprehend.

Everything has been a leap of faith; in the hope of rising again.

Hopefully where I've landed, will see me through to the unknown end.

It is through the image I cast that your brilliance will shine through.

Because the life I've mirrored has been and forever will be...a reflection of you.

Silent Regret

One wrong turn onto Memory Lane, and I break down with regret.

No recollection until I remember what it is I tried to forget.

Approaching a dead end where the bodies I've hidden must now be exhumed.

What I remember and what I've forgotten can only be assumed.

Crimson lights on a winding road warn of the dangers of an oncoming memory.

The morning sun casts shade on this lonely hitchhiker's regret for what has come to be.

I am reminded of choices I've made which caused me to confront my own immaturity.

I tend not to recognize my part nor my unspoken insecurity.

Someone thought I was special and was only trying to impress.

Someone who gave all, as I gave less.

The memories we claim we will cherish forever are stored away until forever forgets,

that the damage of an unfortunate memory is; we shall live with its regrets.

Our remorse permanently changes us just beneath the skin.

However, unlike a tattoo, it is not as easy to cover up our flaws within.

Regret becomes the silence fluttering between the blink of my eyes.

Vacant, dead stares, silently watching as nobody speaks up to advise otherwise.

The voice in my head that could have hit the brakes, and drove me to act more sincere.

When I knew right from wrong but did not choose the path that was clear.

Removing regrets from the forefront of my mind with the use of vices to help them hide.

We conceal our feelings and the decisions we've made, but they will forever abide.

Each fork along the road presents us with different paths to pursue.

But before you get off the main road, take caution, Memory Lane may not be for you.

WINK, BLINK, AND NOD

It happened in a second, and all it took was a wink.

That was all I needed, and it got me to think.

With the close of an eye and the nod of a head,

A smile emerged that could not be misread.

That was all it took, nothing need be said.

That smile tugged at my heart and I felt the love spread.

When your eye opened, I saw things clearer, which made me rethink.

That the rest of my life was waiting there...on the other side of that blink.

SOMETIMES

Sometimes I am the winner, sometimes the loser.

Sometimes I am submissive, sometimes a user.

Sometimes I understand love, sometimes I don't.

Sometimes I'll find love, sometimes I won't.

Sometimes I break away, sometimes I break down.

Sometimes I break through, sometimes I need a break from this town.

But I never actually do break; I seem to know exactly how much I can take.

Sometimes I wonder, sometimes I dream.

Sometimes I annoy, sometimes I scheme.

Sometimes I am masculine, sometimes feminine.

Sometimes I am the omega, sometimes I'm genuine.

Sometimes I am shy, sometimes conniving.

Sometimes I am convincing, sometimes I'm lying.

And I can distinguish the truth from the lies, I can see it there in your eyes.

Sometimes I am relaxed, sometimes irritating.

Sometimes I am loving, sometimes I am frustrating.

Sometimes I agree, sometimes debate.

Sometimes I am on time, sometimes I'm late.

Sometimes I am leaving, sometimes arriving.

Sometimes I am lively, sometimes I am barely surviving.

But I can tell, sometimes I disappoint you, so you must decide what you want to do.

I know who I am and who I can be, and I won't let others decide.

So you must be content to live with the amount of myself that I chose to provide.

Sometimes I'm the sun that lights up your world, sometimes I'm the moon above that shines.

I realize I cannot be everything to you, but I can be something to you, sometimes.

Don't Judge a Book by Its Mirror

When I look in the mirror, I get a glimpse of the real me,

I am not looking at the same person others claim to see.

I'm staring directly into the eyes of my enemy.

I seem to have locked eyes with my personality.

What comes from within is something I can't look past.

Gazing into the mirror and the reflection it casts.

Others see the superficial; I see the supernatural.

But seeing my backstory through my eyes must be contractual.

Should I direct my anger toward a mirror?

The conduit that allows me to see myself clearer.

Frightful of the seven years I could live with its curse.

Will that help or just make it worse?

Possibly one day I could reimagine my story;

and eliminate the scars and blemishes that come from insecurity.

This inner dichotomy is a battle I may never win.My appearance has been overtaken by

the ugly within.

I know this is my autobiography and others believe I overreact.

They don't know this is a work of fiction, I know it is fact.

Each day that passes we add new pages to our journal,

never to be erased, they remain eternal.

My mirror has a story to tell, luckily it will only tell me.

Your story is only told to you, what you conceal, others cannot see.

Our vision of ourselves can become distorted by that mirror on the wall,

Smoke and mirrors can only temporarily give the physical an overhaul.

So if you think you like the way I look, don't peek beyond the cover of my book.

After all, can we ever really be...someone different than the person we all think we see?

MOTHER MAY I...REMIND YOU?

Hopefully, seeing me reminds you of who you were, who you are,

and who I need you to be again, unless it has already gone too far.

You've become more forgetful with each passing year;

The progression is worse than it may appear.

Forgotten are many of the people you once knew.

You have not forgotten me, and I pray you never do.

You're unable to be left alone and unable to fend for yourself.

Your love of reading is a forgotten memory, as are the books on that shelf.

You're unable to take your medication on your own.

And I cannot always be there to ensure you're safe when you're alone.

The tales you tell have begun to unfurl; they've become fantasies of when you were a young girl.

Living in the now, with lucid recollections of the woman you used to be,

All the in-between that made up your life, is now a distant, forgotten memory.

I am unable to remind you of the life you have given us all.

But I'm standing before you today to answer the call.

You are now the one in need of assistance, but you don't know that.

This is not what either of us wanted, but I'll help you adapt.

Regretfully I had to find you a new home, but it is a really nice place;

MARK MY WORDS

Close to me, so I can visit each day, but it allows for your style and grace.

I worry nothing beautiful will come from what you are going through.

But you are healthy, comfortable, and content, so we will have to make do.

It is this damn disease that has taken shelter and lurks in your mind.

But this disease is not how you will be remembered, nor how you'll be defined.

No Room to Roam

There are many rooms inside my home,

The top floor, you are forbidden to roam.

That room is off-limits for others to see,

It is not kept presentable for certain company.

A skeleton key locked that door to eliminate more self-doubt from occupying these halls.

Ever since a previous guest found a way to break through my walls.

I learned at that moment; one may open their home for others to see;

but sometimes your guests cannot live with your debris.

I was left in the dark without the required candlelight.

Someone I cared about had entered, and the flame blew out that night.

Heed my warning, it is best if you just stay out.

Nobody, including you, is free to move about.

For both our sakes, parts of this dwelling I'd prefer you not see.

If the accommodations weren't to your liking, well, that would be the death of me.

Never let my generosity afford you the comfort to explore.

You would not like the person who answers that door.

So turn in for the evening and end your day.

Extinguish the candles that guide your way.

Do not let your curiosity allow you to abandon my hospitality.

As a guest in my home, I have just let you know...where you can and cannot go with me.

LOVE LOST

So here we are; I have lost all respect for you.

Hoping karma is a bitch and you'll get your due.

Pack up your things; I'm going to need you to go.

Like everything else, this too we'll outgrow.

Because of you, I lost my self-respect and dignity.

And since I blame you, I say this spitefully...

No matter what you could do, I no longer believe in us or you.

No matter what you may confess, I couldn't hate you any less.

In case you didn't hear me, by now you should be walking out that door.

I won't even get up to say goodbye and don't forget anything in that drawer.

I can't help but wonder what was up your sleeve.

Fuck all those things we thought we'd achieve.

Stop looking around; there's no love left here, so I need you to leave.

This relationship is dead and it is nothing we need to grieve.

This is all I could do, this is your payback.

Get on the other side of the door and don't look back.

I don't accept your apology and could care less about that tear.

I owe you nothing and as I said before, there is no love left here.

Option #3

Can't you just let it be?

Does it really matter if it was you or me?

Does someone always need to be right?

Would that explain why we continue to fight?

Sometimes it's best not to say a word.

Unspoken sentiments are usually all that are heard.

There is another option we tend to neglect.

Could it possibly be we were both correct?

I know what I feel can't be wrong, although and despite. . .

What you feel is also justified, so you too must be right.

Maybe what we should have learned and what is beginning to show;

is that our feelings are telling us what we should already know.

Perhaps if we listen to ourselves occasionally;

we'd hear that this is not our destiny.

Sometimes you have to feel you belong, to know you belong.

Sometimes you have to go along, to get along.

But we need to move along because we don't belong.

And by the way...I wasn't the one who was wrong.

FIGHTING SPIRIT

As a child, this fort was all I needed, but I knew I'd be drafted for more.

The aspirations I set in youth have become the shortfalls that did not prepare me for war.

Just like this treehouse, my world seems smaller than it was before.

As a child, the world was full of possibilities, yet mine to explore.

Now I search for the ambition to fight for what I wanted before it's too late.

And recover the soul of a life that continues to depreciate.

I must carry out a tactical mission to bridge this inner division.

There is a journey I've yet to take, and I must find the drive within me;

get on the road and change my course or live with what has come to be.

Something better has to be out there somewhere. But without direction, can I find my way there?

I've gathered the necessary intelligence so now is not the time to procrastinate.

I had dreams I'd conquer the world, but when they ended I had nothing to substantiate.

I look at what others have accomplished and I don't compare. How am I still here, how did they get there?

Did I lose it on the battlefields or only in my mind?

I thought I finished my tour of duty, but have since been reassigned.

I was missing in action and eventually a prisoner of my actions.

When the blindfold came off, I was forced to face my delayed reactions.

Now in wartime, I can no longer differentiate friendly fire from enemy lines.

I have been knocked off my feet and therefore I have fallen behind.

But this mission is only halfway complete, and though unprepared, I am not ready to admit defeat.

But what will I do? I'm not really sure. I'm losing the battles, could I still win the war?

The landmines are about to blow. If I give up, can I live with regret when I go?

My fighting spirit will not allow me to quit, for it knows what I want and that this is not it.

I now realize there is so much more to fight for. I may have lost my footing, but I will never be floored.

This will not be the end of the road for me, nor is this as far as my drive takes me.

I am still behind the wheel and what I know for sure is…I have not yet arrived at my destiny.

DOING MY BEST

I've been taught since birth that my life's journey will prove my worth.

I have the need to provide and reassemble what others divide.

I know the evil that men do is not meant to hurt you.

Others often confide in me; they burden me to live with their "something."

Unlike the canary, I have neither the choice nor the voice to sing.

That which I am entrusted with, I am expected to take to the grave.

After all, isn't that what it means to be brave?

A stiff upper lip will utter no gossip.

Ask for proof, even if they've provided the truth.

The third degree will not threaten me.

The hatred visible in the stare of my eyes reflects the origins of all my lies.

One will always see me wearing a smile, for that is the best look for any man's style.

Man was not created to give up before he earns his courage, alone or at war.

He goes into battle to fight for his beliefs and is taught not to waver or bend.

And if his opponent survives, that is when he knows he has found a friend.

So don't think you can get the best of me.

Occasionally someone plays a better game and I'd agree.

But I'll keep moving forward knowing the best is still in front of me.

Even when I am defeated, my best is always...yet to be.

WITCHES BREW

This troublesome day began with a bad cup of coffee.

A sinful roast with enough mystery to convince me; that a cup of java from a local café,

could stir up the beginning of a horrible day.

It is believed the barista cast a spell while percolating that fateful brew.

A cauldron of coffee would serve up a day from hell, brimming with voodoo.

Presto espresso, bad luck it had brought; the rest of the day was to be met with fraught.

Turn back, go home and get into bed; for it would be unwise to forge ahead.

A lack of caffeine and the townsfolk bitching,

made me realize the magic coffee possesses is quite bewitching.

As the day became more malicious, challenges appeared, for which I was not ready.

The hocus pocus was vicious, and my caffeine focus had left me unsteady.

I had enough and the villagers could tell, as the day continued according to spell.

Nobody gave me the slightest break, as the toil and trouble kept brewing.

Extra cream and sugar, couldn't even stop its undoing.

Was it me, was it the coffee, or had they all gone mad?

Abracadabra, I realized it was that rancid potion I had, had.

A sorceress sprinkled bad juju in my java, and the dark arts obeyed.

Fear not, for I knew who could reverse the curse...I'm just not sure if she's a siren or a mermaid.

THE VACANCY

The weep on that willow tree made the obvious hard to see.

But beyond its tears may be the place I've avoided for years.

You needed more, but no sign was on the lawn outside my door.

But while you were gone, my heart became visible, and I would now like to show you around.

At that time, I was not looking to move into what it was you had found.

Now I want to see everything through the warmth of your eyes.

Getting to the heart of the matter will no longer allow for disguise.

I'm committed to making the necessary changes, to become more of your style.

Forgive my manners, I abandoned love and I boarded up the windows with a smile.

At the time I resisted, not knowing a vacancy existed.

Could you still see this for all it can be; a loving place to build and start a family?

I hope by showing you what is in my heart, you will become more aware...

that this could be the perfect fit with the proper love and care.

By your recommendation I have taken down the walls you felt needed to be renovated.

I am hoping this heart-to-heart changes the fact that we have only ever dated.

Regretfully, I shut the door on the life you always dreamed of?

And now it has become clear that I too have fallen in love.

I need you to cross that threshold knowing this is where you belong.

The heart confronts indifference when it can no longer prolong.

And the head must accept what the heart forgives, after all, home is where your heart is.

This was meant to be your home and it always has been.

My heart is open and inviting you to spend the rest of your life within.

THEY

Whenever you were around, I seemed to disappear.

Who I am vanished when your personality was near.

I knew the difference between right and wrong.

I became another nobody to fit in and get along.

You thought I was broken and relished in my despair.

But what you actually think of me, I really do not care.

You rule and reign over those you perceive as weak.

But those are the voices for which I am now about to speak

An eye for an ideology that you would never comprehend.

As the bully, you don't see eye to eye with those who saw you as their friend.

Likewise, you've missed the disdain I had for you when you looked me in the eyes.

My eyes have always spoken for me, and they're incapable of lies.

But the fact that I stood there and said nothing at all,

will cause me regret, as I passively watched the things that I saw.

But learning and growing is the natural law.

And this has only exposed your flaws.

If you ever put anything out there that was even remotely true,

It was a fabrication of events, and your version was selfishly askew.

You have hatred in your heart and it will continue to spread.

The silence I've chosen, allowed you to ignore what I should have said.

The subtle approach did not convey my intentions and that can no longer continue.

You need to abolish the ignorance that lives on within you.

You brought out the worst in me, so my best was not portrayed.

I tried to find the good in you but my efforts were betrayed

I've said enough, and you've heard even less, hopefully, you'll learn one day.

But in the meantime, I will continue to speak up for the "nobodies" you refer to as "they."

THE BLUES

I call her Sky, because I didn't actually catch her name.

A moniker that opposes her cobalt moods, of which no two are the same.

At times I can forecast she'll be sunny and bright.

With a sapphire personality resembling the color of midnight.

In a T-shirt and denim, she is a constant true blue.

I want to go where indigo could not, but she only knows me as "who?"

Her celestial, infectious love of life, cannot be misread.

She won't admit it, but at times she needs help avoiding the peacocks ahead.

She was intriguing and I was intrigued, but I was a cadet she barely knew.

Now I want to see all the various hues that makeup Sky Blue.

What others fail to see, as they try to get to know her...

if you're only using your eyes, the best of someone will be a blur.

Many shades of blue create a turquoise sky, as do the many colors that make up you and

I.

To Hell and Back

I was afraid of the dark, unprepared for the journey on which I was about to embark.

All good comes from up above, but I have been banished down below.

Of course, I am referring to that place you prayed you'd never go.

The entrance is uninviting; it appears I've approached the portal to Hell.

All signs led me to believe this wasn't going to end well.

Another life goes up in flames and like smoke I slither beneath its door.

Inaudible cries of skeletal remains burn to decomposition on the floor.

A charcoal color of darkness and a dank smell fills the air.

All around were telltale signs that goodness and mercy were not there.

My slow descent was calculated by my efforts not to be seen or heard.

The best approach is to be invisible so demon spirits are not stirred.

I realize I've created this hell and it is only mine to fear.

I know I am being watched and I know my end is near.

Who's there? What's that? Both relevant questions when something seems amiss.

I am being punished for my sins and asked, "What did I do to deserve this?"

My heart is stopped by sudden, unfamiliar sounds, the likes of which I've not heard before

My anxiety is suffocated by an evil energy being held captive beneath the floor.

My heightened senses have made me extremely aware.

Hiding in the dark is a presence, although unseen, I know he's there.

Guided by a candle to shed some light only eliminates some of the fright.

MARK MY WORDS

The walls appear to be stained, probably blood.

The floor has been drained, but once plagued by a flood.

I've seen enough and got what I came for, now I must find my way out.

Is that even possible? I guess, I believe, but I doubt.

I can make it out of here. It requires a bolder stance.

I won't let this become my unfortunate circumstance.

All good comes from up above, an act of contrition is my opportunity to survive.

Can I turn this around if I stop heading down and possibly get out of here alive?

I see a light back to salvation. Leading me to believe it was not my time just yet,

I once again danced with the devil and once again won the bet.

Believing in good there is no limit to what can be done. Thanks be to God the Father and his Holy Son.

I was sentenced to Hell and found my way out.

I went through Hell and back for Mom to make spareribs and sauerkraut.

Let's face it, being summoned to get something from the basement at the age of five,

You were kind of left to believe your parents no longer cared...if you're dead or alive.

THE END

I guess I'll always remember the hurtful things you said.

The expressions and words I've tried to erase from my head.

I will walk away crippled by the accusations of you.

This will stigmatize me when I find someone new.

You meant it to hurt me, as I did to you, so that I'd never forget what I put you through.

If I do not return to you, do not think I am dead.

But know that I'm unable to deal with what it is that you said.

You would never know how it hurt to hear, as well as the way that you said it.

For both our sakes, I will not return to you if I cannot bring myself to forget it.

I could just say thank you; it shed light on things that did not make sense.

Now those feelings are clear to me and no longer allow for pretense.

I have no time for talking but let me leave you with this...

The one I love, would not have had to try to become my fantasy,

but would have made me love the person that was standing in front of me.

The person I thought I wanted, was never meant to be the one for whom I belong.

But out there is someone I never thought I wanted, who will become the one I loved all

along.

I guess now is not the time to say, you will continue to hurt me as I go on my way.

I will no longer pretend you're a better person than you are.

I now see you for you, and all your ugly scars.

So let's walk away with these feelings we lack.

Before we do even more damage, let's both end this and get our lives back on track.

AFTERWORD

The one constant in my life has always been music. It has never let me down. It has been with me through good times and bad. It has the potential to remind you of people, places and things that were both good and bad. One song may remind you of a time you were sad and the next may remind you of the good that you have. I love all genres of music and would be honored if someone reads my words one day and hears the potential to turn one of these into a song. I would be up to collaborate if anyone feels they can make something of the words I write.

I am talking to you Bruce, Eddie, Miley, Taylor, Brett, Adam, Post, White, Legend, Orville, Spencer, Bruno, Billie Joe, Father John, Gwen, Alicia, BrOs, Stevie, and yes, definitely you, Adele.

Acknowledgements

Though each of these people are family, or extended family they are also each a friend, and my reason for being. They may never know how much their love and support means to me or that they are my antidote that remedies any of life's challenges.

Thank you for your support in every aspect of my life and in this case, my poetry. I cannot thank you enough or love you more. First I want to thank Talia Scarpato (Cover Artwork) and Evan Dickson (Author Photo) for their contributions to this book and helping me take this journey. I also want to thank those who sat through many impromptu poetry readings and were also supportive of this endeavor, in no particular order: Fallon/Lona, Nina/Jovi, Max/Sandwich, Nancy/BFF, Hailey/Taterbug, Victoria/Victorious, Erin/Rimba, Sal, Shailyn and Ghostlee. Also thanks to the extended family and friends that also allowed me to practice my poetry readings on them: Eric, Maddy, Nick, Denise, Michelle, and Kim. I would also like to thank my Mom, an avid reader and my Dad for his words of encouragement, though both are no longer with me.

~All my Love

Oh, and before I end, I cannot forget to thank Eric Lee and the staff of Holzer Books LLC. For their help and their professionalism.